POT PIES

POT PIES
FORTY SAVORY SUPPERS

BEATRICE A. OJAKANGAS

ILLUSTRATIONS BY SALLY STURMAN

CLARKSON POTTER/PUBLISHERS
NEW YORK

FOR RICHARD OJAKANGAS

Published by Clarkson N. Potter, Inc., 201 East 50th Street, New York, New York 10022. Member of the Crown Publishing Group.

Random House, Inc. New York, Toronto, London, Sydney, Auckland

CLARKSON N. POTTER, POTTER, and colophon are trademarks of Clarkson N. Potter, Inc.

Manufactured in the United States of America

Design by Howard Klein

Library of Congress Cataloging-in-Publication Data
Ojakangas, Beatrice A.
Pot pies : forty savory suppers / Beatrice Ojakangas. — 1st ed.
Includes index.
1. Potpies. I. Title.
TX693.043   1993
641.8′24—dc20   92-16447
CIP
ISBN 0-517-58573-1

1   3   5   7   9   10   8   6   4   2

First Edition

CONTENTS

—■—

INTRODUCTION

Sing a song of sixpence, a pocket full of rye,
Four and twenty blackbirds, baked in a pie . . .

Old cookbooks sometimes explained that a certain crackling, singing sound—like that of a blackbird—indicated that a pie was done. Perhaps this theory inspired the familiar nursery rhyme? While the idea of filling a pie with blackbirds may have been left to the storybooks, the practice of serving main-dish pies fit for a king is still going strong.

Each ethnic group that settled in our country brought its own idea of what should be enclosed in a crust. The main-dish pies of the Greeks, Italians, French, Spanish, Mexican, Finnish, Russian, Moroccans, and English are just a few that are in my repertoire.

Many of these recipes were created as a thrifty way to give leftover meats and vegetables a new life. Even those pies made from scratch are still economical because they make a few ingredients go a long way.

"Pot pies" were originally baked in a pot over an open fire, in a big iron pot—hence their name. The kettle was lined with pastry; filled with meat, potatoes, and vegetables; topped with a second pastry crust; and covered with a lid. It was then slowly cooked in a pit, with a shovelful of hot coals placed over the kettle. Today's pot pies usually consist of a savory filling topped with dumplings, pastry, or sometimes noodles, and are cooked in a conventional oven.

1

In today's hurried world, we often find ourselves eating on the go, consuming food that is unsatisfying and lacking in flavor, nutritional value, and appeal. Pot pies are homey, comforting, and welcome as a casual dinner in front of the fire, a last-minute brunch with friends, or a made-ahead dinner to be reheated after a day on the slopes.

A pot pie's defining characteristic is that it has a crust of some kind. Accompanied by a salad, it can stand as a complete meal. For this book, I have chosen what I consider the most interesting and delicious recipes from hundreds of possibilities. Some have a bottom crust, like the Masa Tart with Ricotta and Goat Cheese, some just a top crust, such as the Chilean Chicken Corn Pie, and some, like Tourtière, are entirely enclosed in crust. The crusts vary from phyllo dough, to whipped potatoes, to those made with cornmeal and masa, to traditional flaky pastry, and you might consider one of the pastries in the final chapter for converting some of your own favorite recipes to irresistible main-dish pies. In the chapters that follow, I have grouped the pies by their fillings rather than by their crusts.

Pot pies can be served for brunch, lunch, supper, or dinner. Many of them make appealing appetizers and first courses when served in small portions, such as the Crab and Mushroom Quiche or Swiss Mushroom Pie. A number of them, Piperade Pie with cheddar crust and the Zucchini Quiche, for example, are great for brunch or lunch, and can be made ahead and reheated before serving. Then there are pies that can turn leftover chicken or turkey into exciting new dishes, such as Chicken and Spinach Pie and Turkey Pie with a Corn Bread Crust. They are all favorites of ours, and can be served not only for family meals but for entertaining as well. Children of all ages seem to love them in particular!

My recipes are straightforward, and with these basic rules and helpful tips, successful pot pies are practically guaranteed:

1. Always use the best-quality ingredients available. If an ingredient is not readily found, use a substitution or, when appropriate, omit it altogether.

2. Read through the recipe before you begin. Check out ingredients, any advance preparation, cooking and cooling times, and the size of the baking dish. Main-dish pies generally require dishes that can go from oven to table.

3. For the best results, use the kind of baking pan specified in the recipe.

TART OR QUICHE PANS may be metal, preferably with a removable bottom. They are usually rather shallow, thus more of the pie's surface is exposed to the heat. If you wish to use a regular pie tin instead, choose one that is slightly smaller—that is, a 9-inch pie tin in place of a 10-inch tart pan, but expect it to take a few minutes more to bake, since a standard pie tin is deeper. If you use a shiny metal pan, place it on a rimless cookie sheet to bake so that the bottom crust will brown evenly. Tart pans usually have a straight scalloped edge that is more attractive than the slanted straight edge of a pie pan.

PORCELAIN OR POTTERY QUICHE PANS usually hold more filling than metal tart pans but may not be deep enough to hold the filling for a deep-dish pie or a pot pie. Always check the volume of the baking pan you are considering, and compare

3

it to the volume specified in the recipe. It is entirely acceptable to use a pan other than the suggested type, but expect a different baking time.

OVEN-TO-TABLE CASSEROLES AND SOUFFLÉ DISHES work very well for many of the pies, again providing they hold the correct volume. They may be made of porcelain, pottery, or glass.

INDIVIDUAL CASSEROLES AND OVENPROOF POTTERY SOUP BOWLS provide a neat way to serve a small group. Simply cover and refrigerate or freeze the remaining servings for another time.

Most pot pies freeze well, especially those with rolled pastry or phyllo crust. After baking, cool them, then wrap them well so that they will not dry out in the freezer and lose flavor. I like to cover the pie first with plastic wrap and then enclose the whole thing in foil. Label and date each dish. I usually slip in a note to myself including the general heating instructions, too, and any ideas or inspirations I might have had about menu accompaniments. If it is convenient, thaw the wrapped pie in the refrigerator, then reheat it, unwrapped, in a slow oven (300°F) until the food reaches serving temperature (140°F to 160°F). Pies can also be frozen unbaked, in which case you can either thaw them before baking, unwrap, and proceed as directed, or put the unwrapped, frozen pies in the oven and allow about 20 extra minutes of cooking time.

PASTRY TECHNIQUES

There are many different pastry possibilities for pot pies, and I've offered a selection ranging from light, fluffy biscuit toppings to flaky pastry crusts. Most of these crusts can be frozen, although the rolled pastries freeze best. Following are two techniques that will help you in your crust preparation.

Prebaking a Pie Shell. Many pot pie recipes call for a partially baked pie shell. To prebake an unfilled crust, roll out ½ of a pastry recipe, and fit it into the appropriate size pan. Crimp the edges decoratively. Line the dough with foil or wax paper and fill with pie weights, uncooked beans, or rice. Bake in a preheated 425°F oven for 12 minutes or until the edges are golden. Remove from the oven and carefully remove the weights and foil. The interior of the pie shell will be pale in color but set, and will bake further with the filling.

Handling Phyllo Dough. Phyllo, sometimes called filo, fila, or strudel leaves, is a tissue-thin pastry dough used in various sweet-and-savory pies of Greek and Middle-Eastern origin. It is readily available in Greek markets and in the frozen foods sections of well-stocked supermarkets.

To use, defrost the phyllo dough at room temperature, still wrapped, for about 2 hours. Remove the pastry from the wrapping and carefully unfold it onto a work surface. Cover with wax paper and a damp tea towel. Remove one sheet of pastry at a time from the stack, keeping the remaining pastry covered so it will not dry out. Phyllo dough is very fragile, so handle it as gently as possible. Wrap any extra pastry immediately, and return it to the freezer.

CHEESE, EGG, AND VEGETABLE PIES

CHEESE AND CHILE PIE

ITALIAN MUSHROOM AND ARTICHOKE PIE

MASA TART WITH RICOTTA AND GOAT CHEESE

PIPERADE PIE

DEEP-DISH SPINACH PIE

FINNISH COUNTRY VEGETABLE PIE

HERBED LEEK AND CHÈVRE TART

SWISS MUSHROOM PIE

RATATOUILLE PIE

RUSSIAN CABBAGE PIE

TORTA RUSTICA

ASPARAGUS TART

ZUCCHINI QUICHE

LENTIL CHILI PIE WITH CORN BREAD CRUST

COUNTRY-STYLE HERBED POTATO PIE

CHEESE AND CHILE PIE

Makes 8 to 12 servings

We have friends of Greek descent who serve crispy little feta-filled phyllo-crusted tarts called *trigona tiropittes* whenever they have a party. I've included the nippy flavor of chopped green chiles and transformed the pastries into a pie, similar to Spanakopita, another favorite Greek specialty. This turned it into a tasty cross-cultural main-dish pie.

18	sheets (¾ pound) phyllo pastry
1	cup crumbled feta cheese
1	cup ricotta cheese
8	ounces cream cheese
1	can (4 ounces) chopped green chiles, drained
¼	cup finely chopped scallions (green onions)
2	eggs, lightly beaten
¼	cup chopped cilantro or fresh parsley
½	cup (1 stick) unsalted butter, melted

Thaw the phyllo as directed on page 5. Preheat the oven to 350°F. Blend the 3 cheeses, chiles, scallions, eggs, and cilantro or parsley to make the filling.

Brush the bottom and sides of a 13 by 9-inch baking pan with melted butter. Place 1 sheet of phyllo on the bottom of the pan; brush lightly with butter. Repeat with 7 more sheets, brushing each lightly with butter, allowing the dough edges to hang over the edges of the pan. Spread half the cheese mixture over the phyllo in the pan. Cover with 7 more sheets of the phyllo, brushing each with butter and folding the edges to fit neatly over the filling. Spread the remaining cheese mixture over evenly. Fold the edges of the bottom sheets over the cheese mixture to encase it. Cover the pie with 3 more sheets of phyllo, brushing each sheet with butter and tucking the edges down inside the pan; brush the top lightly with butter. With a sharp knife, score the top 3 or 4 layers into 8 to 12 sections. (At this point, you can cover and refrigerate the pie until the next day.) Bake, uncovered, for 45 minutes or until golden. If refrigerated, bake an additional 15 to 20 minutes.

Thaw the phyllo as directed on page 5.

Clean and chop the mushrooms. Chop the artichokes, combine them with the mushrooms, and sprinkle the mixture with lemon juice. In a large, nonstick skillet heat 2 tablespoons of the olive oil; add the onions and garlic and cook over medium-low heat for 10 minutes or until the onions are lightly browned. Add the artichokes and mushrooms and cook 25 minutes longer, stirring often. Add the broth in small amounts, waiting until it is absorbed before adding more. Add the parsley and salt and pepper to taste. Remove from heat and set aside to cool.

Mix the ricotta with the eggs, Parmesan, and flour. Blend in salt, pepper, and nutmeg to taste.

Preheat the oven to 375°F. Oil a 10-inch springform pan. Melt the butter and mix with the remaining 2 tablespoons olive oil. Place 1 sheet of phyllo in the pan. Brush lightly with the oil and butter mixture. Repeat this procedure using half of the phyllo sheets, allowing the edges to hang over the sides of the pan. Add the artichoke mixture, then top with the ricotta mixture.

Top the pie with the remaining sheets of phyllo, brushing each sheet with the oil and butter mixture. Gently press all the layers together at the edge of the pan to seal; fold the edges over the center of the pie. Brush with any remaining oil and butter mixture. Bake 40 minutes or until golden. Remove from the oven and cool, uncovered.

Remove the pie from the pan and place on a serving dish. Cut into wedges to serve. Serve hot, warm, or at room temperature.

Masa Tart with Ricotta and Goat Cheese

Makes 6 servings

Masa harina is a specially treated corn flour used in Mexican and Southwestern cooking. In this adaptation of a tart I enjoyed at Tejas, a Southwestern-style restaurant in Minneapolis, masa is substituted for all-purpose flour, resulting in a very tender crust with a delicious corn flavor. Serve wedges of this tart with stir-fried, thinly slivered summer vegetables.

MASA CRUST

1¼	cups masa harina (see Note)
1	teaspoon sugar
½	teaspoon salt
5	tablespoons chilled unsalted butter, sliced in ¼-inch pieces
3 to 4	tablespoons ice water

FILLING

1	cup ricotta cheese
6	ounces goat cheese (chèvre)
2	eggs
2	tablespoons finely chopped chives
1	teaspoon fresh thyme leaves or ½ teaspoon dried
½	teaspoon salt
	Freshly ground black pepper

Tomato salsa
Sour cream or plain yogurt

For the crust, measure the masa harina, sugar, and salt into a bowl. Cut in the butter until the mixture resembles coarse crumbs. Sprinkle the water over and mix just until the dough has the texture of large-curd cottage cheese.

Preheat the oven to 425°F. Press the crumbs firmly onto the bottom and up the sides of a 9-inch tart pan with removable sides. Line with foil. Bake for 12 to 15 minutes or just until the edges begin to brown.

For the filling, whisk together the filling ingredients. Pour the mixture into the partially baked crust. Reduce the oven temperature to 350°F, and bake the pie for 30 to 35 minutes or until the filling is set and a knife inserted just off center comes out clean. Serve in wedges, warm or at room temperature, with salsa and a dollop of sour cream or yogurt.

Note: Masa harina is available at Hispanic or specialty food markets.

PIPERADE PIE

Makes 6 to 8 servings

Piperade is a classic dish of the Basque region of France, made with tomatoes and sweet peppers cooked in olive oil. Ham, bacon, onions, garlic, and other vegetables are often added, and when bound with eggs, the mixture makes a great omelet. Here, I've turned it into a quichelike pie.

½	recipe Lemon Pastry (page 94)
½	cup grated sharp cheddar cheese or aged Swiss cheese
2	tablespoons olive oil
1	small red bell pepper, seeded, stemmed, and coarsely chopped
1	small yellow bell pepper, seeded, stemmed, and coarsely chopped
1	medium onion, coarsely chopped
¼	cup chopped scallions (green onions)
2	garlic cloves, minced or mashed
6	plum tomatoes, peeled, seeded, and chopped
1	tablespoon chopped fresh basil or 1 teaspoon dried
1	teaspoon salt
1	teaspoon freshly ground black pepper
⅛	teaspoon dried red pepper flakes
3	whole eggs, lightly beaten
3	egg whites, lightly beaten

Prebake the pie shell in a 9-inch pie pan (see page 5) and while the crust is still hot, sprinkle the cheese evenly over the bottom. Lower the oven temperature to 350°F.

In a large nonstick skillet, heat the oil. Add the red and yellow peppers, onion, and scallions and cook over medium heat, stirring, for 10 minutes, until soft but not brown. Add the garlic, tomatoes, basil, salt, pepper, and red pepper flakes. Cook 10 minutes or until the liquid evaporates. Cool 15 minutes, then stir in the eggs and spread the mixture in the pastry shell. Bake at 350°F for 30 minutes, until set, or until a knife inserted just off center comes out clean. Serve at room temperature, cut into wedges.

Deep-Dish Spinach Pie

Makes 8 servings

When this square pie is chilled, it is easy to cut into 2-inch squares for appetizers. For a main dish, however, it is best served either hot or at room temperature. Garnish the servings with a dollop of sour cream or plain yogurt and a sprig of fresh basil.

½   recipe Lemon Pastry (page 94)
1   tablespoon Dijon-style mustard
2   pounds fresh spinach, cleaned and stemmed
½   teaspoon dried tarragon
¼   cup fresh lemon juice
1   cup crumbled feta cheese
4   eggs
1½ cups heavy cream or evaporated milk
½   cup sour cream
½   teaspoon salt
¼   teaspoon freshly grated nutmeg

Preheat the oven to 400°F. On a lightly floured surface, roll out the pastry to a 13-inch square and fit into a 9-inch square baking pan. Fold the overhanging pastry all around to make a raised edge and crimp decoratively. Fit a sheet of foil over the dough and fill with pie weights or dried beans.

Bake until the edges are set, about 10 minutes. Remove the foil and weights. Return the crust to the oven and bake 5 to 10 minutes longer, until the bottom is firm and dry.

Brush the pastry with the mustard and return to the oven until set and dry, about 5 minutes. Lower the oven temperature to 375°F.

Put the spinach into a large pot with just the water still clinging to the leaves. Cover and cook over medium-high heat until the spinach is wilted, 2 to 3 minutes. Drain well and chop coarsely. Mix in the tarragon, lemon juice, and feta cheese.

Whisk together the eggs, cream or evaporated milk, sour cream, salt, and nutmeg. Turn the spinach into the partially baked pastry shell and pour the egg mixture over the top. Bake until puffed all over and lightly browned, 45 to 50 minutes. Cool about 15 minutes before cutting.

FINNISH COUNTRY VEGETABLE PIE

Makes 8 servings

When I crave something wholesome, I make this pie. The vegetables must be cooked until they are almost "melted" before they are put into the pastry-lined pan. I've added roasted sunflower seeds, and I serve this pie in wedges with a dollop of sour cream.

The Finnish friend who gave me the original recipe bakes this pie in a deep ovenproof Arabia "chop plate" instead of a tart pan. The chop plate is a standard item in all of the dinnerware designs produced by the Arabia company in Finland.

3	tablespoons butter
2	garlic cloves, minced or pressed
½	cup sliced scallions (green onions), including tops
1	cup shredded parsnip
2	cups shredded carrot
6	cups finely shredded green cabbage
2	cups shredded Emmentaler or provolone cheese
1½	cups cooked brown rice
¼	cup heavy cream
1	teaspoon dried oregano leaves
1	teaspoon salt

¼	**teaspoon ground allspice**
¼	**teaspoon grated nutmeg**
¼	**cup chopped fresh parsley**
1	**recipe Sour Cream Pastry (page 96)**
3	**tablespoons roasted, salted sunflower seeds**
1	**egg, beaten with 2 tablespoons milk, for glaze**

Preheat the oven to 400°F.

In a deep, heavy skillet or wok, heat 1 tablespoon of the butter; add the garlic, scallions, parsnip, and carrot. Cook over high heat for 5 minutes, tossing the mixture constantly so that it will not brown. Add the cabbage; lower the heat to medium and cook, tossing often, until the cabbage is wilted and soft, about 15 minutes. Remove from heat. Add the cheese, rice, cream, oregano, salt, allspice, nutmeg, and parsley. Cool to room temperature.

Roll out two-thirds of the pastry and fit into a 10-inch pie pan or a deep ovenproof platter or tart pan. Mound the cooled filling on the pastry, pressing down until compact. Top with the sunflower seeds and dot with ½-inch slices of the remaining butter.

Roll out the remaining pastry to make an 11-inch circle. Brush with the egg glaze. Cut the pastry into ½-inch-wide strips. Brush the edge of the pastry in the pan with egg glaze. Place the strips over the filling in a latticework pattern. Press the extra strips around the edge of the pie, and crimp if desired.

Bake for 25 to 30 minutes or until the pastry is golden. Serve hot or at room temperature, cut into wedges.

Herbed Leek and Chèvre Tart

Makes 6 servings

If I can get goat cheese, or chèvre, in Duluth, Minnesota, you can probably find it where you live. If not, you can substitute almost any white cheese when making this tart. It won't taste the same, but it *will* be good.

½   **recipe Lemon Pastry (page 94)**
10   **tablespoons (1¼ sticks) butter**
6   **medium leeks, white part and 2 inches of green, cleaned and sliced**
2   **tablespoons white wine vinegar**
½   **teaspoon salt**
½   **teaspoon freshly ground black pepper**
½   **cup heavy cream**
7   **ounces goat cheese (chèvre)**
2   **tablespoons minced fresh chives**
½   **cup fresh bread crumbs**
2   **tablespoons minced fresh chervil or parsley**

Prebake the pastry shell in a 9-inch pie pan (see page 5), and lower the oven temperature to 350°F.

In a large skillet, melt ½ cup (1 stick) of the butter. Add the leeks and cook over medium heat, stirring, until wilted, about 5 minutes. Add the vinegar, salt, and pepper. Reduce the heat to low and cover; cook until leeks are very soft and tender, about 35 minutes. Increase the heat to high and add the cream. Cook, stirring, until the cream is absorbed, about 1 minute. Remove from heat and cool.

Crumble the goat cheese over the bottom of the cooled tart shell. Top with the leek mixture, mounding it slightly in the center. Sprinkle the mixture with the chives and bread crumbs. Dot with ¼-inch cubes of the remaining butter. Bake the tart until golden brown and heated through, about 15 minutes. Garnish it with the chervil or parsley. Serve warm or at room temperature.

SWISS MUSHROOM PIE

Makes 8 servings

I blend the crumbs for this easy press-in crust in the food processor and prebake it while preparing the filling. A slice of this pie, either hot or cold, makes a nice lunch with a green salad.

SWISS CHEESE PRESS-IN CRUST

1	cup all-purpose flour
6	tablespoons chilled butter, sliced ¼-inch thick
½	cup shredded aged Swiss cheese
¼	cup sour cream

MUSHROOM FILLING

1	tablespoon butter or vegetable oil
2	small garlic cloves, minced
1	pound fresh brown (Cremini) or white mushrooms, cleaned
1½	cups shredded aged Swiss or Emmentaler cheese
1	teaspoon salt
½	cup light cream or milk
2	eggs, lightly beaten

Preheat the oven to 425°F. For the crust, measure the flour into a large bowl. Cut in the butter until the mixture resembles coarse crumbs. Blend in the cheese and sour cream until the mixture resembles moist crumbs. Press the crust into a 9-inch glass or porcelain quiche pan or pie pan. Bake it for 10 minutes or until lightly browned.

For the filling, heat the butter in a heavy skillet; add the garlic and stir over low heat for 2 minutes. Add 8 mushroom caps to the pan and cook just until glazed, 1 to 2 minutes; remove them and reserve. Slice the remaining mushrooms with stems and add to the pan. Cook and stir until the mushrooms are browned and any released liquid has evaporated. Sprinkle half the cheese over the baked crust. Top the cheese with the mushrooms, then the remaining cheese. Mix the salt, cream, and eggs, and pour into the pan, covering the ingredients evenly.

Bake for 25 to 30 minutes or until a knife inserted just off center comes out clean. About 5 minutes before removing the pie from the oven, place the reserved mushroom caps on top of the pie, spacing them evenly around the edge. Serve the pie hot or at room temperature. The pie can be baked a day ahead, refrigerated, and warmed in a 300°F oven for 10 minutes before serving.

Ratatouille Pie

Makes 8 servings

Ratatouille is a popular Provençal dish of vegetables, garlic, and herbs simmered in olive oil. Bound by a ricotta-egg custard and baked in a wheat-cracker crust, it becomes a great main-dish pie served hot or at room temperature.

2	cups whole-wheat cracker crumbs
4	tablespoons (½ stick) unsalted butter, melted
½	cup freshly grated Parmesan cheese
2	tablespoons olive oil
3	small garlic cloves, minced or pressed
1	medium onion, coarsely chopped
3	medium zucchini, cut in ¼-inch slices
1	small (1 pound) eggplant, cut in ½-inch dice
2	small bell peppers (1 red and 1 green), diced
¼	cup chopped fresh basil or parsley
1	cup ricotta cheese
2	eggs
1	teaspoon salt
3	ripe tomatoes, peeled, seeded, and diced

Preheat the oven to 375°F. For the crust, mix the cracker crumbs and butter. Press two-thirds of the mixture into a 10-inch pie pan. Spread the remaining crust mixture in another pan. Bake the crumb-lined pie pan and extra crumbs for 10 minutes or just until toasted, shaking the extra crumbs once during baking. Sprinkle the warm pie crust with ¼ cup of the Parmesan cheese and cool.

In a large, heavy skillet, heat the olive oil. Add the garlic and onion and cook for 2 to 3 minutes, stirring, until the onion is soft. Add the zucchini, eggplant, and bell peppers and cook and toss over high heat for 10 minutes. Add the basil or parsley. Stir the ricotta, eggs, and salt together, and blend them into the vegetable mixture. Turn into the crumb-lined pan. Sprinkle the top with the remaining Parmesan cheese and the toasted crumbs.

Bake for 20 to 25 minutes or until the pie is set. Before serving, sprinkle with the diced tomatoes. Serve hot or at room temperature.

Russian Cabbage Pie

Makes 6 servings

For the best flavor, the cabbage needs to be cooked over low heat until it is very soft and sweet tasting.

3   tablespoons butter
1   medium onion, thinly sliced
1   small head green cabbage, trimmed and finely shredded (about 3 cups)
1   teaspoon dried basil
1   teaspoon dried marjoram
1   teaspoon dried tarragon
1   teaspoon salt
½   teaspoon freshly ground black pepper
½   pound fresh mushrooms, cleaned and sliced
1   recipe Lemon Pastry (page 94)
1   package (3 ounces) cream cheese, at room temperature
4   hard-cooked eggs, sliced
1   teaspoon dried dill

In a large, heavy skillet, melt 2 tablespoons of the butter. Add the onion and cabbage, and cook over medium-low heat, turning with a spatula until the cabbage is wilted, about 5 minutes. Sprinkle with the basil, marjoram, tarragon, salt, and pepper. Continue cooking another 10 to 15 minutes or until soft but not browned. Remove from the pan. Add the remaining butter to the skillet, then add the mushrooms and cook, stirring, over medium heat, until the mushrooms are soft and the liquid has evaporated, 5 to 6 minutes.

Preheat the oven to 375°F. Roll out two-thirds of the pastry and fit it into a 9-inch square pan. Spread the pastry with the cream cheese and top with the sliced eggs. Sprinkle with the dill. Top evenly with the cabbage, then top the cabbage with the mushrooms.

Roll out the remaining pastry and fit it onto the top of the pie. Moisten and flute the edges to seal. Make a few short slashes for vents. Bake for 25 to 30 minutes or until the crust is golden brown. Serve warm or at room temperature.

TORTA RUSTICA

Makes 12 servings

This is a wonderful pie to have in your repertoire for a picnic or for hot summer evenings. It tastes great and slices easiest when made ahead and chilled, but the flavor is best after it has returned to room temperature. I like to serve wedges of this colorful pie with a dollop of freshly made pesto.

½   **pound fresh mushrooms, thinly sliced**

1   **small sweet onion, chopped**

3   **tablespoons olive oil, plus oil for pan**

20   **ounces fresh spinach, cleaned**

¼   **cup chopped fresh Italian flat-leaf parsley**

1   **tablespoon chopped fresh basil or 1 teaspoon dried**

½   **teaspoon freshly ground black pepper**

12   **eggs, lightly beaten**

½   **cup oil-packed sun-dried tomatoes, drained and chopped**

1   **recipe Quick-Rising Pizza Dough (page 99)**

½   **cup freshly grated Parmesan cheese**

¾   **pound provolone cheese, shredded**

¾   **pound thinly shaved Italian sausage, such as mortadella, salami, pepperoni, or prosciutto (optional)**

1   **egg yolk, mixed with 1 tablespoon milk, for glaze**

In a 10-inch, nonstick skillet over medium heat, cook the mushrooms and onion in 1 tablespoon of the olive oil until the mushrooms are tender, about 5 minutes. Turn up heat to high and add the spinach by a handful at a time, cooking each handful until it wilts. When all the spinach is wilted, remove the vegetables from the pan using a slotted spoon. Boil any remaining liquid down until 2 to 3 tablespoons remain. Pour the liquid over the vegetable mixture; add the parsley, basil, and pepper. Set aside.

In the same nonstick skillet, heat 1 tablespoon more olive oil over medium-high heat. In a bowl, mix the eggs with the tomatoes. Add half the egg mixture to the heated pan. Make an omelet, lifting up the edges of the cooked eggs with a spatula and letting the uncooked portion flow under, until the eggs are barely set. Turn the omelet out onto a plate. Heat the remaining oil and repeat to make a second omelet.

Preheat the oven to 375°F.

On a lightly floured surface, roll out ¾ of the pizza dough to make a large circle about ¼ inch thick. Oil a 10-inch springform pan and place the dough in the pan, covering the bottom and sides of the pan. Sprinkle the dough with half of the Parmesan cheese, half of the provolone, half of the sausage (if used), and half of the spinach-mushroom filling. Top with one omelet, the remaining spinach filling, the second omelet, and the remaining sausage (if used), provolone, and Parmesan.

Roll out the remaining dough into a circle to fit the top of the pie. Place on the pie and pinch the edges of the dough to seal. Pierce with a sharp knife to make vents. Brush with the egg-milk glaze.

Place the springform pan on a baking sheet and bake for 1 hour to 1 hour and 15 minutes, until the top is browned. If the crust begins to brown excessively, cover with foil during the last half hour of baking. Cool on a rack. Cover and chill at least 4 hours for best slicing.

ASPARAGUS TART

Makes 6 servings

Serve this tart for breakfast or brunch. Make it a day in advance and reheat it in a 350°F oven for 10 to 15 minutes.

½	**recipe Lemon Pastry (page 94)**
1½	**pounds fresh asparagus, cleaned and trimmed**
4	**ounces cream cheese, at room temperature**
3	**eggs**
1	**cup heavy cream**
¾	**teaspoon salt**
½	**teaspoon freshly ground pepper**
¼	**pound thinly sliced prosciutto or shaved ham, cut into ⅛-inch strips**
⅓	**cup freshly grated Parmesan cheese**

Fit the pastry into a 10-inch tart pan with a removable bottom. Trim the edges and place in the freezer for 10 minutes.

Cut 2½ inches off the asparagus tips and cut the stems into 2-inch pieces. Blanch the asparagus in boiling water for 2 minutes, just until crisp-tender. Drain and plunge them into cold water to stop the cooking. Drain well.

Preheat the oven to 425°F. Blend the cream cheese, eggs, cream, salt, and pepper until smooth.

Arrange the sliced asparagus stalks and ham on the pastry. Pour in half the egg mixture. Bake 15 minutes, then remove from the oven. Add the remaining egg mixture and arrange the asparagus tips on top of the pie. Sprinkle with the Parmesan cheese. Reduce the oven temperature to 375°F and bake for 40 minutes or until a knife inserted just off center comes out clean. Cool 15 minutes before serving in wedges, either warm or at room temperature.

ZUCCHINI QUICHE

Makes 6 to 8 servings

This is perfect for a summertime Sunday brunch served with sausages and a platter of fresh fruit.

½	recipe Lemon Pastry (page 94)
¼	cup freshly grated Parmesan cheese
¼	cup shredded sharp cheddar cheese
½	cup seasoned dry bread crumbs
2	eggs, separated
1½	cups sour cream
2	tablespoons chopped chives
2	tablespoons all-purpose flour
1	teaspoon salt
½	teaspoon freshly ground black pepper
1½	pounds zucchini, cut in ¼-inch slices

Roll out the pastry to fit into an 11-inch tart pan with a removable bottom.

Preheat the oven to 450°F. Mix the cheeses with the bread crumbs. Sprinkle ½ cup of the mixture evenly over the bottom of the pastry.

Beat the egg yolks, sour cream, chives, flour, salt, and pepper together. Beat the egg whites until stiff and fold into the yolk mixture.

Arrange one-third of the zucchini slices over the cheese mixture in the pastry-lined pan. Cover with one-third of the sour cream mixture. Repeat layering until the zucchini and egg mixture are used up.

Bake for 10 minutes; reduce the oven temperature to 325°F and bake for 40 minutes more or until the pie is set. Cool for at least 15 minutes and cut into wedges to serve, either warm or at room temperature.

LENTIL CHILI PIE WITH CORN BREAD CRUST

Makes 8 servings

This delicious, spicy vegetable chili can be made ahead, actually becoming more flavorful over two or three days. Be sure the chili is good and hot before you turn it into a deep casserole and top with the corn bread batter.

1	large onion, chopped (about 2 cups)
¼	cup vegetable oil
2	garlic cloves, minced or pressed
2	tablespoons chili powder
2	teaspoons ground cumin
1	teaspoon dried oregano
1	teaspoon dried thyme
1	teaspoon paprika
⅛	teaspoon dried red pepper flakes
5	cups chicken broth
2	cups lentils, picked over and rinsed
1	can (14 ounces) whole tomatoes, chopped, including juice
2	bell peppers (1 green and 1 yellow), chopped
3	celery stalks, chopped
1	recipe Corn Bread Crust (page 97)

In a Dutch oven or deep, heavy pot, cook the onion in the oil for 10 minutes over low heat. Add the garlic, chili powder, cumin, oregano, thyme, paprika, and pepper flakes; cook, stirring, for 3 minutes. Stir in the chicken broth, lentils, and tomatoes; simmer 40 minutes; add up to 1 cup water if the mixture becomes dry. Add the bell peppers and celery, and simmer for 15 minutes longer. (At this point the chili can be cooled and refrigerated.) Turn the chili into a 3-quart deep casserole (reheat first if refrigerated).

Preheat the oven to 400°F. Drop the Corn Bread Crust batter by spoonfuls over the chili. Bake for 30 minutes or until a wooden pick inserted into the corn bread comes out clean.

COUNTRY-STYLE HERBED POTATO PIE

Makes 6 to 8 servings

Use Idaho Russets in this pie for the best results. Note that the first baking is done without the egg and cream custard, which is added through a hole in the top crust after the potatoes are tender. Sliced tomatoes with a basil vinaigrette are the perfect accompaniment.

1	recipe Lemon Pastry (page 94)
2	tablespoons chopped fresh chives
2	tablespoons chopped fresh chervil
2	tablespoons chopped fresh basil
2	tablespoons chopped fresh parsley
2	pounds baking potatoes, peeled and sliced ⅛ inch thick (6 cups)
1	cup shredded Emmentaler or Swiss cheese
6	ounces cooked ham, cut into ½ x 4-inch slices
½	teaspoon salt
½	teaspoon freshly ground black pepper
2	tablespoons butter, cut into ½-inch pieces
1	egg, beaten with 1 teaspoon water, for glaze
2	egg yolks
½	cup heavy cream

Roll out half the pastry and fit it into a 9-inch pie pan. Preheat the oven to 425°F.

In a small bowl, combine the herbs and set aside. Layer one-third of the potatoes in the pie shell; sprinkle with one-third each of the herbs, cheese, and ham. Sprinkle each layer lightly with salt and pepper. Repeat layering. Dot the top with butter. Roll out the remaining pastry to fit the top. Moisten the edges with the egg glaze and seal. Cut a ½-inch round hole in the center of the pastry to make a vent, insert a small metal funnel, then brush the crust with the egg glaze.

Bake for 30 minutes, then reduce the temperature to 350°F for 20 to 30 minutes, until the potatoes are tender.

Beat the egg yolks and cream. Pour the mixture into the funnel in the pastry. Remove the funnel and shift the pan to distribute the cream. Bake about 10 minutes longer. Cool at least 10 minutes before slicing.

CHICKEN, TURKEY, AND SEAFOOD PIES

CHICKEN POT PIE WITH ROASTED PEPPERS

CHICKEN AND SPINACH PIE

CHILEAN CHICKEN CORN PIE

MOROCCAN CHICKEN PIE

SCALLOP, ROASTED PEPPER, AND
MUSHROOM POT PIE

CRAB AND MUSHROOM QUICHE

SALMON–WILD RICE PIE

SHRIMP PIE WITH DILLED HAVARTI AND
ROASTED PEPPERS

SEAFOOD GUMBO PIE

TURKEY PIE WITH A CORN BREAD CRUST

THANKSGIVING IN A PIE

SAVORY TURKEY-BROCCOFLOWER PIE

CHICKEN POT PIE WITH ROASTED PEPPERS

Makes 6 servings

Cooking a chicken whole with bell peppers in a searingly hot oven develops a rich flavor. Often, I roast the chicken and peppers a day ahead of time before adding them to the mushroom sauce. I also bake the pastry crusts ahead and add them to the pie just before serving so that they stay crisp.

1	**(3- to 3½-pound) whole chicken**
2	**bell peppers (1 red and 1 yellow)**
1	**recipe Lemon Pastry (page 94)**
1	**large sweet onion, sliced thickly**
½	**pound fresh mushrooms, cleaned and sliced**
2	**tablespoons all-purpose flour**
1	**cup dry white wine**
1	**cup chicken broth**
½	**cup heavy cream**

Preheat the oven to 450°F. Wash and dry the chicken and place it in a roasting pan along with the peppers. Roast for about 40 minutes, turning the peppers once, until the skins are blistered. Remove the peppers and place them in a brown paper bag. Cook the chicken 5 to 10 minutes longer, then cool. Tear the meat into shreds, discarding the skin and bones, and place in a bowl. Drain off and reserve any juices that accumulate.

Cover and refrigerate the chicken and juices separately.

When the peppers are cool, peel off the skins, remove the stems and seeds, and cut into 1-inch strips; refrigerate. (You can prepare the recipe to this point up to a day ahead.)

Preheat the oven to 425°F. For a large pie, divide the pastry into 2 parts. Roll each part out to the diameter of a 1½-quart shallow baking (or soufflé) dish. Place the pastry circles on a cookie sheet and pierce all over with a fork. Bake at 425°F until golden, 20 to 25 minutes. Cool and reserve.

Remove the hardened fat from the juices. Measure 2 tablespoons of the broth into a skillet. Cut the onion rings into quarters and add with the mushrooms to the skillet. Cook over medium heat, stirring occasionally, for 10 minutes, until the onion is tender. Sprinkle with the flour. Stir in the wine, chicken broth, and cream; bring to a boil and cook, stirring, until the sauce is thickened. Add the chicken and peppers and cook until heated through.

Place one of the baked pastry rounds in the bottom of the baking dish. Spoon in the filling and bake for 15 to 20 minutes, until bubbly. Top with the second pastry. Serve immediately.

For individual pies: Roll out the pastry to ¼-inch thickness. Cut twelve 5-inch rounds and place them on a cookie sheet. Pierce each one with a fork in 4 or 5 places. Bake for 10 to 12 minutes, until golden. Cool and reserve.

Place each baked pastry round in the bottom of individual casseroles or ovenproof soup bowls. Spoon the filling into the pots and bake the casseroles for 15 minutes or until bubbly. Top each casserole with a baked pastry round. Serve immediately.

CHICKEN AND SPINACH PIE

Makes 6 to 8 main-dish servings
or 10 to 12 appetizer wedges

This is a wonderful pie—a bit garlicky, a bit sweet with raisins—and when sliced cold it reveals a beautiful mosaic of spinach, chicken, and pine nuts. Reheat wedges for a quick snack, lunch, supper, or appetizer.

2   **packages (10 ounces each) frozen chopped spinach, or 3 pounds fresh, washed and trimmed**
2   **large garlic cloves, minced or pressed**
¼   **cup raisins**
¼   **cup pine nuts or slivered blanched almonds**
¼   **pound thinly sliced prosciutto or ham, slivered**
1   **tablespoon olive oil**
1   **tablespoon unsalted butter**
3   **cups shredded cooked chicken**
2   **eggs, lightly beaten**
1   **cup heavy cream or evaporated milk**
    Salt and freshly ground black pepper
1   **recipe Cornmeal Pastry (page 98)**

Cook the spinach according to package directions, or, if using fresh, chop the spinach and place it in a pot with just the water that clings to the leaves. Cook, stirring occasionally, over medium-high heat for 3 to 5 minutes, until wilted. Drain and squeeze out as much liquid as possible. Mix the spinach with the garlic, raisins, nuts, and prosciutto.

Heat the oil and butter in a skillet over medium-high heat. Add the spinach mixture. Cook, stirring, until the garlic and nuts begin to color, about 5 minutes. Turn the mixture into a bowl. Add to the bowl the chicken, eggs, cream, and salt and pepper to taste.

Preheat the oven to 350°F.

Roll out two-thirds of the pastry and fit it into a 9-inch pie pan. Turn the filling into the pastry. Roll out the remaining pastry to fit the top of the pan. Moisten the edges of the pastry in the pan. Place the top pastry over the pie and press together the edges to seal. Make several slashes on the top of the pie. Bake until the pastry is golden brown, and the center of the pastry is set, 45 to 55 minutes.

CHILEAN CHICKEN CORN PIE

Makes 6 to 8 servings

This spicy chicken pie has a top "crust" of a baked corn-kernel omelet. Remember this one if you have leftover cooked turkey, too.

1	**medium onion, chopped**
1	**garlic clove, minced or pressed**
2	**tablespoons (¼ stick) butter**
2	**tablespoons all-purpose flour**
1	**cup chicken broth**
¾	**teaspoon chili powder**
3	**cups cooked chicken or turkey, cubed or shredded**
½	**cup pitted black olives, sliced**
¼	**cup raisins**
2	**cups corn kernels (fresh, frozen, or canned), drained**
½	**cup milk**
1	**egg, lightly beaten**
½	**teaspoon salt**

Preheat the oven to 350°F. Butter a 1½-quart casserole.

In a heavy skillet cook the onion and garlic in 1 tablespoon of the butter over medium heat for 3 to 4 minutes, until soft. Stir in 1 tablespoon of the flour and the chicken broth. Cook, stirring until thickened, then add the chili powder, chicken, olives, and raisins. Spoon into the prepared casserole.

Combine the corn, 1 tablespoon melted butter, 1 tablespoon flour, milk, beaten egg, and salt. Spoon the custard mixture over the chicken mixture. Bake the pie for 35 minutes or until bubbly. Meanwhile, preheat the broiler. Then place the pie in the broiler and broil until the top is flecked with golden brown spots, a few minutes.

MOROCCAN CHICKEN PIE

Makes 8 servings

This is an adaptation of *bastilla* (or *bisteeya*), the classic Moroccan chicken pie that is seasoned with aromatic spices and wrapped in phyllo. To eat Moroccan style, plunge your fingers into the pastry and lift out pieces of the spicy chicken filling. Hot mint-flavored tea is the traditional accompaniment.

1	(3- to 3½-pound) chicken, quartered
1	large onion, chopped
2	large garlic cloves, chopped
1	tablespoon turmeric
1	tablespoon ground cinnamon
1	teaspoon ground ginger
1	teaspoon ground cumin
1	teaspoon ground allspice
½	teaspoon ground cloves
½	teaspoon ground mace
½	teaspoon ground coriander
½	teaspoon ground dried thyme
6	cups chicken broth
½	cup chopped fresh parsley
6	eggs, lightly beaten
¼	cup (½ stick) butter, melted
8	sheets (¼ pound) phyllo dough
1	tablespoon granulated sugar mixed with 1 teaspoon ground cinnamon, for sprinkling

1   cup finely ground almonds, plain or blanched
Confectioners' sugar and ground cinnamon

Put the chicken with the giblets in a large (5- to 6-quart) pot. Add the onion, garlic, spices and thyme, and the chicken broth. Heat to boiling. Cover and simmer until the chicken pulls from the bones easily, 1 to 1¼ hours.

Remove the chicken from the broth, reserving the liquid. Cool. Discard the skin and bones, then shred the meat into bite-size pieces. Heat the reserved broth to boiling. Add the parsley, and pour the eggs into the broth, stirring until curds form. Pour the mixture into a strainer set over a bowl and let stand until well drained. Reserve the broth for another use.

Preheat the oven to 425°F. Brush a 10-inch pie pan with melted butter. Arrange 6 sheets of the phyllo dough in the pan, brushing each sheet with butter as you stack it. Overlap them to cover the bottom, allowing the dough to extend 6 to 8 inches beyond the rim of the pan. Sprinkle with the cinnamon-sugar mixture and top with the shredded chicken. Spread the egg mixture over the chicken and top with the almonds. Fold the phyllo over the filling, and brush with butter. Fold the remaining 2 sheets of phyllo in half crosswise and place on the pie, tucking the edges inside the pan. Brush with butter. Bake, uncovered, for 20 minutes, until golden.

Shake the pan to loosen the pie; hold a baking sheet loosely over the top of the pie and invert the pan. Lift off the pan. Bake 10 minutes longer, until golden. Invert the pie onto a platter and let stand for 5 minutes. Sift the confectioners' sugar generously over the top and sprinkle with cinnamon.

Scallop, Roasted Pepper, and Mushroom Pot Pie

Makes 6 servings

This flavorful scallop stew is topped with flaky pastry rounds. You can make the stew a day ahead; before serving, simply reheat it in the oven and top with pastry.

2	medium bell peppers (1 red and 1 yellow)
½	recipe Lemon Pastry (page 94)
2	tablespoons olive oil
1	tablespoon butter
1½	pounds large sea scallops
2	garlic cloves, minced
1	pound mushroom caps (reserve stems for another use)
1	cup sliced scallions (green onions), in 1-inch pieces, including green part
3	tablespoons all-purpose flour
¼	cup dry white wine
½	cup heavy cream
	Fresh lemon juice
	Salt and freshly ground black pepper to taste

Preheat the oven to 500°F. Wash the peppers and place them on a cookie sheet in the oven. Roast 20 minutes or until the peppers are blistered on all sides, turning them once. Transfer the peppers to a paper bag and let them stand for 15 minutes. Peel and seed the peppers, then cut them into 1-inch squares. Reduce the oven temperature to 375°F.

Roll the pastry into a 12-inch circle. Using 2½-inch round cookie cutters, cut 6 circles. Transfer the rounds to a baking sheet, prick them several times with a fork, and bake for 10 to 12 minutes or until golden.

Place half the oil and half the butter into a skillet over high heat. Add the scallops and toss, cooking for 15 to 30 seconds. Add the garlic, tossing just until the scallops are white and springy to the touch, about 5 minutes. Remove the scallops with a slotted spoon and reserve. Reduce the juices to a glaze, then add the mushroom caps and scallions. Cook, stirring, until the mushrooms and scallions are well coated and the mushrooms have released their liquid, about 3 minutes; remove with a slotted spoon and reserve.

Cook down the juices to a glaze again, and add the remaining oil and butter; sprinkle in the flour. Whisk in the wine and cream and any juices from the reserved scallops and mushrooms; cook until thickened and smooth. Add the scallops, mushrooms, and peppers. Add the lemon juice, salt, and freshly ground pepper to taste.

Turn the mixture into a 1½-quart casserole, or divide among 6 individual casseroles or shallow ovenproof soup bowls. Bake for 10 minutes for individual casseroles, 20 minutes for a large pie, or until just heated through. Top with the baked pastry rounds. Serve at once.

CRAB AND
MUSHROOM QUICHE

Makes 8 servings

This recipe lends itself well to variation. If I have a lot of bits and ends of various kinds of cheeses on hand, I substitute them for the Swiss cheese. Sometimes I include herbed cream cheese, such as Boursin, in place of part of the cottage cheese.

½ recipe Lemon Pastry (page 94)
2 tablespoons (¼ stick) butter
½ pound fresh mushrooms, cleaned and sliced
4 eggs
1 cup sour cream
1 cup small-curd low-fat cottage cheese
½ cup freshly grated Parmesan cheese
¼ cup all-purpose flour
¼ teaspoon salt
 Freshly ground black pepper
 Freshly grated nutmeg
4 drops hot pepper sauce
2 cups shredded Swiss cheese
½ pound lump crabmeat, picked over

Partially prebake the pastry in a 9-inch porcelain quiche pan or a 10-inch pie pan (see page 5). Lower the oven temperature to 350°F.

In a heavy skillet, heat the butter and sauté the mushrooms until they are tender and the liquid has evaporated, 5 to 10 minutes.

In a large bowl, blend the eggs, sour cream, cottage cheese, Parmesan cheese, flour, salt, pepper, nutmeg, and hot pepper sauce.

Sprinkle half the Swiss cheese into the pastry shell. Top with the mushrooms and crabmeat. Spoon the cottage cheese mixture over and top with the remaining Swiss cheese. Bake for 45 minutes or until a knife inserted near the center comes out clean. The quiche should be puffed and lightly browned. Let it stand for at least 5 minutes before cutting into wedges. Serve hot or at room temperature.

SALMON–WILD RICE PIE

Makes 6 to 8 servings

Salmon pies are a Finnish favorite. For appetizers, I sometimes fill little rounds of pastry with the mixture, just like filled cookies.

1	recipe Lemon Pastry (page 94)
2	tablespoons butter
3	scallions (green onions), cleaned and chopped
½	pound fresh mushrooms, cleaned and chopped
1	teaspoon salt
1	teaspoon dill weed or dried thyme leaves
2	cups cooked wild rice
3	large eggs
4	cups cooked, boned, and flaked salmon
1	cup sour cream, plus additional to serve (optional)

GLAZE

1	large egg
1	tablespoon milk or water

Preheat the oven to 400°F. Roll out half of the pastry on a lightly floured surface and fit it into a 9- or 10-inch quiche pan or pie pan.

In a heavy, nonstick skillet, melt the butter over medium heat. Add the scallions and mushrooms and cook, stirring occasionally, for about 5 minutes, or until the scallions are tender and the mushrooms are soft. Remove the pan from the heat and cool.

Stir the salt, dill, wild rice, and 1 lightly beaten egg into the cooked vegetables. Turn the mixture into the pastry-lined pan. In a medium-sized bowl, lightly beat the 2 remaining eggs and mix them gently with the salmon. Spread the mixture evenly over the wild rice mixture in the pan. Spread the sour cream evenly over the top.

Roll out the remaining pastry and fit it over the filling. Fold the edges over and crimp to seal well.

For the glaze, mix the ingredients and brush over the top of the pie. Pierce the top all over with a fork and bake the pie for 35 to 40 minutes or until golden. Serve warm or at room temperature with a dollop of sour cream (if used).

SHRIMP PIE WITH DILLED HAVARTI AND ROASTED PEPPERS

Makes 6 to 8 servings

Danish Dilled Havarti cheese imparts a creaminess and subtle herby flavor to this quichelike shrimp pie.

½   recipe Lemon Pastry (page 94)
2   teaspoons Dijon-style mustard
1   cup diced Danish Dilled Havarti cheese
¾   pound medium shrimp, cooked, shelled, and deveined
3   scallions (green onions), thinly sliced
1   cup half-and-half or light cream
3   large eggs
1   yellow bell pepper, roasted, seeded, and sliced (see Note)
1   red bell pepper, roasted, seeded, and sliced (see Note)

Preheat the oven to 400° F. Roll out the pastry on a lightly floured surface and fit it into a 9-inch pie pan; flute the edges. Brush the bottoms and sides of the pastry with the mustard. Scatter half the cheese on the pastry, top evenly with the shrimp, then sprinkle on the remaining cheese and the scallions.

In a bowl, whisk together the cream and eggs; pour over the filling.

Arrange the yellow and red bell peppers decoratively over the top of the pie and press into the creamy mixture slightly.

Bake for 30 minutes or until a knife inserted in the center of the pie comes out clean. Serve hot or at room temperature.

Note: To roast the peppers, preheat the oven to 500°F, line a baking pan with foil, and place the whole peppers on the foil. Bake for about 15 minutes, turning once, until the peppers are blistered. Remove the peppers from the oven and place them in a brown paper bag. Close the bag and allow to stand for 15 minutes. Peel off the peppers' skin, cut them in half, and remove the seeds and stems. Cut the peppers into thin lengthwise slices.

SEAFOOD GUMBO PIE

Makes 6 to 8 servings

With the addition of a light and tender buttermilk biscuit topping, gumbo becomes a wonderful pot pie. An authentic gumbo starts with a rich and dark mahogany roux, made by browning flour in oil. An easier, fat-free way to brown the flour is to toast it in the oven. Although it isn't as authentic, I sometimes substitute either fresh or frozen asparagus for the okra.

FILLING

½	**cup all-purpose flour**
2	**tablespoons (¼ stick) butter**
2	**garlic cloves, minced or pressed**
1	**cup chopped onion**
1	**cup diced celery, in ¼-inch cubes**
½	**cup chopped green bell pepper**
½	**cup chopped red bell pepper**
½	**pound andouille or other smoked pork sausage, thinly sliced**
½	**pound julienned cooked ham**
2	**cups chicken broth**
¾	**pound uncooked shrimp, shelled and deveined**
½	**pound lump crabmeat, picked over**
½	**pound fresh okra, sliced, or 1 package (10 ounces) frozen cut okra**
1	**teaspoon gumbo filé or dried thyme**
½ to 1	**teaspoon hot pepper sauce**

2   **teaspoons fresh lemon juice**
    Salt and freshly ground black pepper

BUTTERMILK BISCUIT CRUST

2   **cups sifted cake flour**

2   **teaspoons baking powder**

2   **teaspoons sugar**

½   **teaspoon baking soda**

½   **teaspoon salt**

6   **tablespoons (¾ stick) cold unsalted butter, cut in ¼-inch slices**

½   **cup plus 1 or 2 tablespoons buttermilk**

1   **tablespoon butter, melted**

Preheat the oven to 400°F.

For the filling, spread the flour in a shallow baking pan and bake for 12 to 15 minutes, stirring or shaking frequently until well browned. Be careful not to let the flour burn. Set aside.

In a large, nonstick skillet, melt the butter; add the garlic, onion, celery, and peppers and cook over medium heat until the vegetables are tender, about 10 minutes. Add the sausage and ham. Sprinkle the browned flour over and mix until all ingredients are coated with the flour. Add the chicken broth and heat to boiling. Simmer 15 minutes, until the mixture is thickened. Add the shrimp, crabmeat, okra, and gumbo filé or thyme. Cook, stirring, over medium-high heat for 2 to 3 minutes or until shrimp is pink. Add the hot pepper sauce, lemon juice, and salt and pepper to taste. (At this point, you may cover and refrigerate the gumbo until the next day. If refrigerated, reheat the gumbo to simmering before proceeding.)

Preheat the oven to 425°F. Turn the mixture into a shallow 2½-quart casserole and set aside.

For the crust, combine the flour, baking powder, sugar, baking soda, and salt in a large bowl. Cut in the butter until the mixture resembles coarse crumbs. Stir in ½ cup buttermilk just until a dough forms; add 1 to 2 more tablespoons if necessary.

On a floured surface, roll the dough out until ½ inch thick. With a 2½-inch round cookie cutter, cut out rounds and arrange on top of the gumbo. Brush the biscuits with the melted butter. Bake until the filling is bubbly and the biscuits are golden and light, 20 to 25 minutes.

Note: Turkey ham and sausages are now widely available and can be substituted for the red meat versions.

TURKEY PIE WITH A CORN BREAD CRUST

Makes 8 servings

This is a comforting, cold-weather kind of dish, perfect for the weekend after Thanksgiving when there may still be remnants of the holiday feast in the refrigerator. You can substitute almost any cooked vegetables for those called for in the recipe, and chicken can be used in place of the turkey.

2   tablespoons (¼ stick) butter
2   medium onions, thinly sliced
⅓   cup all-purpose flour
3   cups hot turkey or chicken broth
     Salt and black pepper to taste
⅛   teaspoon hot pepper sauce
4   cups cubed cooked turkey
2   cups diced cooked carrots
2   cups diced cooked potato
1   cup baby lima beans, fresh or frozen
1   recipe Corn Bread Crust (page 97)

Preheat the oven to 425°F. Butter a 3-quart casserole.

In a heavy, deep skillet or saucepan, melt the butter. Add the onions and cook over low heat, stirring often, until softened but not browned, about 15 minutes. Whisk in the flour, then the hot broth. Heat to boiling and cook until thickened. Taste and add salt, pepper, and hot pepper sauce.

Layer the turkey, carrots, potato, and lima beans in the casserole. Pour the sauce over the ingredients, then spoon the crust batter evenly over the turkey and vegetables. Bake until the crust is golden on top and a toothpick inserted in the center comes out clean, 35 to 40 minutes. Serve immediately.

THANKSGIVING IN A PIE

Makes 10 main-dish or 20 appetizer servings

This pie makes an ideal candidate for a picnic or a spectacular presentation on a buffet table. Its dramatic layers and holiday flavors make it a very popular offering.

1   **recipe Flaky Cottage Cheese Pastry (page 95)**
2   **tablespoons whole-grain mustard**

TURKEY PÂTÉ

1   **garlic clove, peeled**
1   **pound ground turkey**
1   **large egg**
1   **teaspoon salt**
½   **teaspoon freshly ground black pepper**
¼   **teaspoon ground allspice**
¼   **teaspoon ground nutmeg**
2   **tablespoons brandy**

TURKEY LAYER

1½   **pounds cooked smoked turkey, thinly sliced**
2   **tablespoons whole-grain mustard**
2   **tablespoons brandy**

STUFFING

¼   **cup (½ stick) butter**
1   **small onion, minced**
1   **teaspoon dried thyme leaves**
½   **cup chicken broth**
2   **tablespoons chopped fresh parsley**

1   **large egg**
8   **slices whole wheat bread, crumbled**

CRANBERRY LAYER

12   **ounces fresh cranberries, picked over**
1   **cup water**
1   **cup sugar**

Preheat the oven to 300°F. Roll out the pastry on a lightly floured surface and then fit it into a 10-inch springform pan. Crimp the edges decoratively and brush the bottom and sides with the mustard.

For the pâté, combine all of the ingredients in a food processor fitted with the steel blade and process until smooth. Spread the mixture evenly on the mustard-lined pastry.

For the turkey layer, top the pâté evenly with half the turkey slices. Brush the turkey with 1 tablespoon of the mustard and sprinkle with 1 tablespoon of the brandy.

For the stuffing, melt the butter in a skillet; add the onion and sauté over medium heat until the onion is soft, about 10 minutes. Add the thyme, broth, parsley, egg, and bread and blend well. Pack the stuffing on top of the turkey layer in the pan. Top the stuffing with the remaining turkey slices, then brush with the remaining mustard, and sprinkle on the remaining brandy.

Insert a meat thermometer into the center of the pie so that the tip is in the pâté. Cut a 10-inch circle of parchment or waxed paper and fit it on top of the pie, allowing the thermometer to run through the paper. Bake the pie for 2 hours or until the thermometer registers 165°F. Cool thoroughly.

For the cranberry layer, while the pie bakes, combine the cranberries, water, and sugar in a saucepan; bring to a boil over medium heat and cook, stirring occasionally, for 10 minutes, until thickened. Remove from heat and cool.

Spread the cranberry mixture on top of the cooled pie. Chill the pie until the cranberry layer is set, about 4 hours. Serve cold or at room temperature, cut into wedges.

SAVORY TURKEY-BROCCOFLOWER PIE

Makes 6 to 8 servings

Sometimes called "broccoflower," green cauliflower is now available in the produce sections of many supermarkets. Its flavor is sweet like cauliflower, but hints of broccoli as well. You can substitute either of its cruciferous cousins, broccoli or cauliflower, in this pie, one of my favorites.

1	recipe Sour Cream Pastry (page 96)
1	head green cauliflower, in florets (about 4 cups)
4	tablespoons butter
¾	pound ground turkey breast
2	garlic cloves, minced or pressed
4	tablespoons all-purpose flour
1	cup chicken broth
1	cup light cream or milk

1   teaspoon salt
1   teaspoon dried thyme leaves
1   teaspoon Dijon-style mustard
1   tablespoon sherry
1   cup shredded Swiss cheese

Preheat the oven to 425°F. Divide the pastry into two parts, one slightly larger than the other. Roll out the larger part on a lightly floured surface and fit it into a 9 × 1¼-inch round quiche pan or a 10-inch pie pan. Place the pan and the remaining pastry, wrapped in plastic, in the refrigerator while preparing the filling.

Steam the cauliflower florets until tender, 8 to 10 minutes. In a heavy, nonstick skillet, melt 1 tablespoon of the butter over medium heat and brown the turkey until cooked through, 5 to 8 minutes. Remove the turkey from the pan and reserve.

Add the remaining butter and the garlic to the pan. Stir over medium heat until the garlic is fragrant, 1 to 2 minutes. Stir in the flour and cook for 2 minutes, stirring. Slowly whisk in the chicken broth, light cream, salt, thyme, mustard, and sherry. Continue stirring over medium heat until the sauce is smooth. Remove from heat.

Sprinkle the cheese evenly over the bottom of the chilled pastry-lined pan. Top the cheese with the turkey mixture, then the green cauliflower. Pour the sauce over the filling.

Roll out the remaining crust and fit it over the pie. Moisten and seal the edges, and crimp decoratively.

Bake the pie in the preheated oven for 30 to 35 minutes or until golden brown. Cool slightly. Cut into wedges to serve.

Meat Pies

FIESTA BEEF PIE WITH CORNMEAL PASTRY

FLEMISH BEEF PIE CARBONNADES

HAM AND CHEESE PIE

LAYERED HAM AND VEGETABLE PIE
WITH CABBAGE-LEAF CRUST

VENISON POT PIE

TAMALE PIE

FRENCH EASTER PIE

PORK POT PIE WITH PEPPERED
CORN BREAD CRUST

SPICED SHEPHERD'S PIE WITH
FETA-POTATO TOPPING

PICNIC PIE

TOURTIÈRE

RUSTIC DEEP-DISH PIZZA

PIZZA POT PIE

Fiesta Beef Pie with Cornmeal Pastry

Makes 6 servings

Southwestern? Tex-Mex? However you would classify this pie, it has an enticing flavor and festive color. To make it ahead of time, either make the filling and the pastry and refrigerate them separately, then assemble and bake the pie before serving; *or* assemble the whole pie, then wrap and freeze it. If frozen, add another 25 to 30 minutes to the baking time.

1	tablespoon corn oil
1	pound lean boneless beef top round steak, in ½-inch cubes
½	cup chopped red bell pepper
½	cup chopped green bell pepper
½	cup chopped onion
½	pound fresh mushrooms, cleaned and sliced
1½	cups chunky bottled tomato salsa
2	cups fresh or frozen corn kernels
2	teaspoons sugar
1	teaspoon chili powder
½	teaspoon ground cumin
1	teaspoon salt
½	cup sliced pitted black olives
1	recipe Cornmeal Pastry (page 98)
1	egg, beaten, for glaze

Heat the oil in a large, heavy skillet. Add the meat and cook until well browned; remove the meat to a bowl. In the drippings, cook the peppers, onion, and mushrooms until tender. Add the salsa, corn, sugar, chili powder, cumin, salt, and cooked beef; heat to boiling. Reduce the heat to low, cover, and simmer 30 minutes, stirring the mixture occasionally. Remove from heat, and stir in the olives.

Preheat the oven to 425°F. Divide the crust into 2 parts, and roll out half the dough to fit into a 9- or 10-inch pie or quiche pan. Spoon the filling into the pie shell. Roll the remaining dough out slightly larger than the top of the pie. Brush the edges with beaten egg. Place the dough circle on top of the pie, fold the top edge under the bottom crust, and flute the edges to seal. Brush the top with the remaining egg glaze. Bake for 35 minutes or until the meat filling is hot and crust is golden.

FLEMISH BEEF PIE CARBONNADES

Makes 8 servings

Dark beer is responsible for the rich flavor of this beef stew, which, topped with a crust of whipped potatoes, is quite pretty on a buffet table.

4	pounds lean beef stew meat, in 1½-inch cubes
1	tablespoon vegetable oil
2	garlic cloves, halved
1	tablespoon all-purpose flour
¼	tablespoon freshly ground black pepper
2	bottles (12 ounces each) dark beer
¼	cup red wine vinegar
3	tablespoons Dijon-style mustard
3	bay leaves
½	teaspoon thyme leaves, crumbled
2	tablespoons (¼ stick) butter
4	large onions, sliced into ¼-inch rings
8	carrots, cut into ½-inch cubes
4	tablespoons potato starch, arrowroot, or cornstarch

WHIPPED POTATO CRUST

2	pounds potatoes, peeled and halved
2	tablespoons (¼ stick) butter, melted
½	teaspoon salt

¼	teaspoon freshly ground pepper
½ to ¾	cup milk, heated
2	egg whites

| 2 | tablespoons (¼ stick) butter, melted, for top of pie |

Pat the beef dry. Heat the oil in a nonstick skillet; add the garlic and about one-third of the meat. Brown the meat over high heat, stirring constantly. Remove the meat to a Dutch oven or deep casserole. Brown the remainder of the meat in batches. Sprinkle the browned meat with the flour and pepper. Add about 1 cup of the beer to the skillet and heat to boiling, scraping up the browned bits from the bottom. Add the vinegar, mustard, bay leaves, and thyme. Pour the liquid over the meat mixture along with an additional 1¼ cups of the beer.

Melt the butter in the same skillet over medium-high heat. Add the onions and cook, stirring, until golden brown, about 7 minutes. Add the onions to the meat and heat to simmering. Cover and cook over low heat until the meat is tender, about 2 hours. Add the carrots during the last 30 minutes of cooking. When the meat is done, blend an additional ¼ cup of beer with the starch (½ cup beer will be left over). Stir into the stew and cook until thickened, 3 to 5 minutes. (You can prepare the pies up to this point 2 to 3 days ahead and rewarm the stew to finish the pie.)

For the crust, put the potatoes into a saucepan and add salted water to cover. Bring to a boil and simmer until tender, about 20 minutes.

Drain the potatoes and transfer to a large bowl. Beat with a mixer at medium speed until potatoes are mashed and smooth. Beat in the melted butter, salt, and pepper. Gradually beat in the hot milk until potatoes are light and fluffy. Beat the egg whites until stiff but not dry, then gently fold the whites into the potatoes.

Preheat the broiler. Reheat the stew, if refrigerated. Taste and adjust the seasoning. Transfer the stew to a broiler-proof serving dish or shallow casserole. Spoon the hot potatoes into a pastry bag fitted with a star tip and pipe the potatoes on top of the stew. Drizzle with the melted butter. Broil 6 inches from the heat until lightly browned, and serve immediately.

HAM AND CHEESE PIE

Makes 6 to 8 servings

This is a great pie to make when you have leftover cooked ham after a holiday meal. My husband takes chilled wedges of it in his lunchbag, and it's just delicious served with a freshly grated horseradish sauce or crème fraîche flavored with curry.

½   **recipe Lemon Pastry (page 94)**
1   **tablespoon coarse-grain mustard**
1   **tablespoon butter**
1   **cup chopped fresh mushrooms**
1   **cup chopped scallions (green onions)**

¼   **cup chopped fresh parsley**

½   **cup heavy whipping cream or undiluted evaporated milk**

1   **cup shredded provolone or mozzarella cheese**

¼   **cup freshly grated asiago, Parmesan, or Romano cheese**

3   **large eggs, lightly beaten**

2   **cups (¾ pound) ground cooked ham, turkey ham, or smoked turkey breast**

1   **large tomato, cut into 12 wedges**

Roll out the pastry and fit it into a 9- or 10-inch quiche pan or pie pan. Prebake it as directed on page 5

Brush the inside of the baked shell with the mustard. Preheat the oven to 350°F.

In a large, nonstick skillet over medium heat, melt the butter and sauté the mushrooms and scallions for 5 minutes, or until tender.

Turn the vegetables into a mixing bowl and add the parsley, cream, half of the shredded provolone or mozzarella, the grated asiago, eggs, and ham. Mix well.

Turn the filling into the pie shell and smooth the top.

Bake for 35 to 40 minutes, until a knife inserted in the center of the pie comes out clean. Remove the pie from the oven and arrange the tomato wedges over the top. Sprinkle with the remaining shredded cheese. Return to the oven for 5 to 10 minutes longer, until the tomatoes are hot and the cheese is melted. Serve chilled, room temperature, or warm, cut in wedges.

LAYERED HAM AND VEGETABLE PIE WITH CABBAGE-LEAF CRUST

Makes 8 servings

Succulent layers of pureed vegetables and cubes of smoked ham, all enclosed in blanched cabbage leaves, make a very tasty pie. Turkey ham or smoked turkey breast can be used in place of the ham for those who prefer not to use red meat.

1   (1½ pounds) green cabbage, cored
3   tablespoons butter, plus additional melted
     butter to serve (optional)
2   garlic cloves, minced or pressed
1   large leek (white and light green parts only),
     cleaned and thinly sliced
3   eggs, lightly beaten
1   teaspoon salt
½   teaspoon freshly ground black pepper
¼   teaspoon ground nutmeg
3   potatoes (about 1 pound), peeled, cooked, and
     mashed
1   pound carrots, peeled, cooked, and mashed
1   pound ham, diced in ¼-inch pieces

Preheat the oven to 350°F. Butter a 2-quart round casserole or soufflé dish.

Bring a large pot of water to a boil. Add the cabbage head and cook, lifting the cabbage out of the water occasionally to peel off and drain the large outer leaves as they loosen. Trim off any tough ribs.

In a large skillet, melt 1 tablespoon of the butter over medium heat, then add the garlic and leek. Cook, stirring occasionally, until the leek is soft, about 10 minutes. Turn the mixture into a bowl and mix in the eggs, salt, pepper, and nutmeg. Add half of the mixture to the mashed potatoes and mix well. Add the remaining half of the mixture to the mashed carrots and blend well.

Line the bottom and sides of the prepared casserole with cabbage leaves, using 4 to 8 leaves. Reserve 4 to 8 whole cabbage leaves to cover the top of the pie. Finely chop and drain the remaining cabbage. Sprinkle the bottom of the casserole with ½ of the ham cubes; cover with the potato mixture and then a layer of chopped cabbage. Top with the carrot mixture and the remaining ham. Top with the reserved cabbage leaves. Dot with the remaining 2 tablespoons butter. Bake the pie for 1½ hours or until it feels firm in the center when pressed lightly. Serve hot with melted butter (if used).

VENISON POT PIE

Makes 8 servings

When my brothers, avid hunters, bring me venison in the fall, I make this hearty and spicy pot pie. It is equally appealing made with beef. The stew improves as it stands, making it a convenient dish to serve after a day of cross-country skiing. I make the filling and the crust ahead, refrigerate them, then assemble and bake the pie as we enjoy appetizers and a sauna.

1	**tablespoon butter**
1	**tablespoon olive oil**
2	**pounds venison or beef stew meat, in ½-inch cubes**
½	**cup all-purpose flour**
2	**cups chopped onions**
2	**cups diced carrots**
2	**cups diced rutabaga, turnip, or kohlrabi**
3	**cups dry red wine**
3	**cups beef broth**
3	**tablespoons chopped fresh sage or 1 tablespoon dried**
2	**bay leaves**
3	**tablespoons Special Spice Mix (see Note)**
1	**large potato, peeled and diced**
	Hot pepper sauce to taste
	Worcestershire sauce to taste

1   **recipe Lemon Pastry (page 94)**
1   **egg, lightly beaten with 1 tablespoon water,
       to glaze**

Heat the butter and oil in a large, heavy Dutch oven over medium heat. Dredge the meat in the flour and brown in batches, transferring to a bowl as you go. Add the onions, carrots, and rutabaga to the pan, then brown over high heat for 3 minutes. Remove and reserve. Add the wine to the pan and boil until reduced by half. Return the venison to the pan. Add the beef broth, sage, bay leaves, and Special Spice Mix. Simmer, covered, for 1 hour. Add the browned vegetables and potato, and simmer 30 minutes. Add the hot pepper and Worcestershire sauces.

Preheat the oven to 350°F. Turn the filling into a 3-quart casserole. Roll the crust out to fit the top of the pan and press the edges to the pan. Trim off any excess. Brush the pie with glaze, and pierce 4 or 5 times to make air vents. Bake for 35 to 45 minutes or until the crust is golden. Serve hot.

Note: To make Special Spice Mix, combine 3 tablespoons paprika, 2 tablespoons powdered garlic, 2 tablespoons black pepper, 1 tablespoon onion powder, 1 tablespoon oregano, 1 tablespoon thyme leaves, and 2 teaspoons salt. Store in a jar with a tight-fitting lid.

Good

TAMALE PIE

Makes 6 servings

Mexican tamales are little "pies" wrapped in corn husks and steamed. Tamale Pie is a simplified main-dish pie baked in a casserole. The flavors are much the same, but this version is much simpler and quicker to make, and of course, you don't have to hunt for corn husks!

2	**teaspoons corn oil**
1	**garlic clove, minced or mashed**
1	**medium onion, chopped**
1	**small green pepper, chopped**
½	**pound lean ground beef**
½	**pound lean ground pork**
1	**can (28 ounces) whole tomatoes, chopped, including juices**
1	**cup corn kernels (fresh, frozen, and thawed or canned), drained**
1	**teaspoon salt**
¼	**teaspoon black pepper**
2	**tablespoons chili powder**
¼	**cup yellow cornmeal**
½	**cup sliced, pitted black olives**

CORNMEAL TOPPING

1½	**cups milk**
½	**teaspoon salt**
2	**tablespoons (¼ stick) butter**

½   cup yellow cornmeal
1   cup shredded cheddar cheese
2   eggs, lightly beaten

Heat the oil in a large, preferably nonstick skillet and add the garlic and onion; cook over medium-high heat for 2 minutes or until soft. Add the pepper and meats; cook, stirring, until the meat is cooked through. Add the tomatoes, corn, salt, pepper, and chili powder. Sprinkle the cornmeal over and stir into the mixture until blended. Add the olives and turn into a 2-quart casserole.

For the topping, heat the milk, salt, and butter to scalding in a heavy saucepan. Gradually whisk in the cornmeal. Cook, stirring, until thickened. Remove from heat and stir in the cheese and eggs.

Preheat the oven to 375°F. Spread the topping over the casserole. Bake for 25 to 30 minutes or until the topping is golden and puffy. Serve immediately. *Good c̄ Sour Cream*

Try a wider casserole dish, rather than a deep one. Also, should have room at top when filling it spills over while baking.

FRENCH EASTER PIE

Makes 6 servings

Follow the directions for cutting the pastry when you make this pie, and it will end up in the oval shape of an egg. With an artistic hand, you can make fancy cutouts to decorate the egg.

1½	**pounds lean ground pork**
3	**tablespoons chopped fresh parsley**
1½	**teaspoons salt**
1	**teaspoon freshly ground black pepper**
1	**teaspoon thyme leaves**
¼	**teaspoon ground allspice**
1	**recipe Lemon Pastry (page 94), chilled**
4	**hard-cooked eggs, peeled and halved**
1	**egg, beaten, for glaze**

Combine the ground pork, parsley, salt, pepper, thyme, and allspice.

Preheat the oven to 325°F. Cover a baking sheet with parchment paper or lightly grease it.

Roll two-thirds of the pastry into a rectangle 8 by 12 inches and about ⅛ inch thick. Cut off the corners to form an 8-sided piece of pastry. Place on the prepared baking sheet.

Spread half the meat mixture in the middle of the pastry, leaving a 2-inch border. Place the hard-cooked eggs on top with the cut side down, then mound the remaining filling on top.

Roll out the remaining pastry, and cut to make a similar 8-sided shape. Place over the filling, and moisten, pinch, and seal the edges, rounding the corners to make an oval shape. Make 2 or 3 slits in the lid and brush with the beaten egg. Roll out the pastry scraps and cut them into fancy shapes. Place them on top of the pie. Brush again with the egg and bake for 1 hour or until golden. Remove the pie from the oven and cool to room temperature.

Pork Pot Pie
with Peppered
Corn Bread Crust

Makes 6 generous servings

There's a lot of flexibility to this recipe. Season it up or down using your favorite chili recipe as a guide. Bake it either in individual portions or in a 2½-quart dish. You can make the meat mixture ahead and refrigerate it a day or so before adding the biscuitlike cornmeal topping. Chilled, it will take a few extra minutes to bake. A great cold-weather dish!

1½	pounds lean ground pork
1	cup chopped onion
1	large bell pepper, chopped
1	can (15 ounces) tomato sauce
2	tablespoons tomato paste
1	package (10 ounces) frozen corn kernels, thawed
1	tablespoon cornmeal
1	tablespoon Worcestershire sauce
1	tablespoon ground cumin
1	tablespoon chili powder
1	teaspoon hot pepper sauce, or more to taste
½	teaspoon ground allspice

PEPPERED CORN BREAD CRUST

1   cup all-purpose flour
1   cup yellow cornmeal
3   tablespoons sugar
2   teaspoons baking powder
3   tablespoons butter, melted
¾   cup milk
1   egg, lightly beaten
½   cup shredded Monterey Jack cheese
1   can (4 ounces) green chili peppers, chopped
       and drained

In a large, heavy, preferably nonstick skillet, brown the pork with the onion and bell pepper until the pork is cooked. Stir in the tomato sauce, tomato paste, corn, cornmeal, Worcestershire sauce, cumin, chili powder, hot pepper sauce, and allspice. Simmer for 30 minutes, stirring occasionally. Spoon the mixture into 6 individual pots or into one 2½-quart casserole. (Refrigerate at this point if desired.)

Preheat the oven to 400°F. For the crust, stir the flour, cornmeal, sugar, and baking powder together in a large mixing bowl. Stir the butter, milk, and egg together in another bowl, and add to the dry ingredients; stir until just blended. Stir in the cheese and chili peppers.

Drop large spoonfuls of the crust mixture onto the pork mixture. Bake for 10 minutes. Reduce the oven temperature to 350°F, and bake for 30 minutes longer or until the filling bubbles and the crust is lightly browned.

SPICED SHEPHERD'S PIE WITH FETA-POTATO TOPPING

Makes 8 servings

The original shepherd's pie is an unpretentious combination of ground cooked lamb mixed with leftover gravy and onions, and topped with mashed potatoes. This recipe is a little more exciting, with a decidedly Greek flair!

1	tablespoon olive oil
2	garlic cloves, minced or pressed
1	large onion, chopped
2	pounds lean ground lamb
2	teaspoons crumbled dried mint
1	teaspoon ground cinnamon
1	teaspoon oregano leaves
½	teaspoon ground allspice
4	plum tomatoes, peeled, seeded, and chopped
	Salt and freshly ground pepper to taste
¼	cup freshly grated Parmesan cheese

FETA POTATO TOPPING

6	large potatoes, peeled and cubed
2	tablespoons (¼ stick) butter
	Salt and black pepper to taste
¼	cup freshly grated Parmesan cheese
2	cups feta cheese, crumbled

In a large, heavy skillet, heat the olive oil. Add the garlic and onion and cook for 1 minute. Add the lamb and cook, stirring, until the lamb is no longer pink. Drain off any excess fat. Add the mint, cinnamon, oregano, allspice, tomatoes, and salt and pepper. Stir in the Parmesan cheese.

Butter a 2-quart casserole and turn the mixture into it. (You may cover and refrigerate the mixture at this point.)

Preheat the oven to 400°F. For the topping, put the potatoes into a pot with water to cover. Cook for 15 to 20 minutes or until tender. Drain, reserving some of the liquid. Beat with an electric mixer, adding the butter, salt and pepper, and enough cooking liquid so that the potatoes become fluffy. Blend in the Parmesan and feta cheeses. Spoon the potato mixture over the lamb mixture in the casserole. Bake for 35 to 40 minutes or until lightly browned.

PICNIC PIE

Makes 8 servings

Encased in a golden crust, this well-seasoned ground-meat pie is perfect for a picnic or a leisurely supper, served with a green salad.

1	tablespoon butter
1	medium onion, chopped
2	garlic cloves, minced or pressed
½	cup dry white wine
1	pound ground veal, turkey, or very lean beef
½	pound ground ham or turkey ham
½	cup soft bread crumbs
½	cup chopped fresh parsley
1	egg
½	teaspoon salt
½	teaspoon thyme leaves
½	teaspoon ground allspice
½	teaspoon dry mustard
1	recipe Lemon Pastry (page 94)
1	egg, lightly beaten, for glaze

In a heavy skillet, melt the butter over medium heat. Add the onion and garlic, and cook for 5 minutes, until the onion is soft. Add the wine. Bring to a boil and cook, stirring, until the liquid has evaporated, about 8 minutes, then turn the vegetables into a large bowl. Add the ground meats, bread crumbs, parsley, egg, salt, thyme, allspice, and dry mustard, blending well.

Preheat the oven to 375°F. Roll out two-thirds of the pastry to fit into an 8-inch springform pan. Spoon the meat mixture evenly into the crust. Roll out the remaining pastry to fit the top of the pan. Moisten the edges, trim any excess, and seal the edges. Roll out the scraps and cut into decorative shapes. Brush the top of the pie with beaten egg. Place the pastry cutouts on top, and brush again with egg. Slash the top to make vents.

Bake for 1 hour or until browned. Cool for 15 minutes. Serve warm, cut into wedges.

TOURTIÈRE

Makes 8 servings

Tourtière is a traditional French Canadian meat pie served at the midnight meal following Christmas Eve mass. It is a great make-ahead dish for family or entertaining during the holiday season. Serve it hot, room temperature, or cold; offer with a variety of mustards.

1	pound lean ground pork
1	pound lean ground beef
1	large onion, chopped
1	garlic clove, minced
2	whole cloves
2	tablespoons chopped fresh parsley
2	tablespoons chopped celery leaves
1	teaspoon salt
¼	teaspoon freshly ground black pepper
⅓	cup fine cracker crumbs
1	recipe Lemon Pastry (page 94)
	Milk, for brushing top

In a wide skillet, cook the ground meats, onion, garlic, cloves, parsley, celery, salt, and pepper, stirring, until the meat is cooked, about 20 minutes. Taste and adjust the seasoning. Add the cracker crumbs and cool slightly. Discard the cloves.

Preheat the oven to 450°F. Divide the pastry into 2 parts. Roll out one half to fit a 10-inch pie pan. Spoon the meat mixture into the crust. Roll out the remaining pastry and place over the filling; trim and seal the edges. Brush the top of the pastry with milk. Roll out the pastry scraps and cut into shapes. Place them on top of the pie and brush again with milk. Slash the top to make vents. Bake for 15 minutes, then lower the heat to 350°F and bake until the crust is golden, 15 to 20 minutes longer. Cut into wedges, and serve hot or at room temperature.

Rustic Deep-Dish Pizza

Makes 8 servings

I bake this pizza in a 10-inch springform pan, but you can use a regular "deep dish" pizza pan as large as 12 inches in diameter. The pizza dough hangs over the sides of the pan, and once filled, you fold the edges over the top of the pie to make a very rustic-looking pie.

1	**pound bulk Italian-style sausage**
1	**large onion, minced**
2	**teaspoons chopped fresh basil leaves**
2	**teaspoons chopped fresh oregano leaves**
1	**teaspoon fresh thyme leaves**
½	**teaspoon freshly ground black pepper**
1	**cup chopped fresh plum tomatoes, seeded**
1	**recipe Quick-Rising Pizza Dough (page 99)**
1	**cup shredded mozzarella cheese**
¼	**cup freshly grated Asiago or Parmesan cheese**
¼	**cup chopped fresh parsley**
	Olive oil

Crumble the sausage into a heavy, nonstick skillet; add the onion and cook over medium-high heat, stirring occasionally, until the meat is cooked through and the onion is tender, about 5 minutes. Add the basil, oregano, thyme, pepper, and tomatoes. Heat the mixture to boiling and cook until the liquid has evaporated, about 5 minutes. Turn into a bowl and cool.

Preheat the oven to 375°F. Oil a 10-inch springform pan that is 2½ to 3 inches deep. On a floured surface, roll out the dough into a 20-inch circle. Carefully fit the dough into the prepared pan so that the edges overhang equally all around. Spoon the meat filling into the center and spread to the edges of the pan. Sprinkle with the mozzarella, Asiago or Parmesan, and parsley. Fold the overhanging dough over the filling, leaving a hole in the center. Brush the top with olive oil and bake for 35 to 45 minutes, until golden brown. Serve hot or at room temperature, cut into wedges.

PIZZA POT PIE

Makes 6 to 8 servings

This is a deep-dish pizza that's baked with the thick crust on top. Layers of cheese, meat, and fresh vegetables meld together beneath to create a real crowd pleaser!

½	**pound extra-lean ground beef**
½	**cup chopped onion**
2	**garlic cloves, minced**
1	**cup sliced fresh mushrooms**
½	**pound pepperoni, diced into ¼-inch cubes**
12	**ounces fresh spinach leaves, cleaned**
1	**tablespoon chopped fresh basil or 1 teaspoon dried**
½	**teaspoon dried oregano leaves**
⅛ to ¼	**teaspoon red pepper flakes**
1	**cup shredded mozzarella cheese**
½	**cup freshly grated Parmesan cheese**
½	**pound meaty plum tomatoes, seeded and thinly sliced**
1	**recipe Quick-Rising Pizza Dough (page 99)** **Olive oil**

In a heavy, nonstick skillet over medium-high heat, sauté the beef, onion, 1 garlic clove, and the mushrooms until the meat is browned and the mushrooms are tender, about 4 minutes. Add the pepperoni and stir to combine. Turn the mixture into a 10-inch-deep pie pan and spread it in an even layer.

Place the same skillet over high heat and add the remaining clove of garlic, and the spinach leaves. Cover and cook until the spinach is wilted, about 2 minutes. Remove from heat and add the basil, oregano, and red pepper flakes. Mix well and spread in an even layer over the meat in the pie pan. Top with the mozzarella and half the Parmesan. Cover evenly with the tomato slices, and sprinkle the remaining Parmesan on top.

Preheat the oven to 375°F. Roll out the pizza dough and place on top of the ingredients in the pan, tucking in the edges all around. Pierce with a sharp knife to make vents and brush with olive oil. Bake for 35 to 45 minutes, until the crust is golden. Serve hot.

BASIC PASTRIES FOR PIES

LEMON PASTRY

FLAKY COTTAGE CHEESE PASTRY

SOUR CREAM PASTRY

CORN BREAD CRUST

CORNMEAL PASTRY

QUICK-RISING PIZZA DOUGH

LEMON PASTRY

Makes enough pastry for 1 double-crust pie

This is one of my all-time favorite pastries for pies. The combination of egg and lemon juice makes it tender and flaky.

2	cups all-purpose flour
½	teaspoon salt
¾	cup (1½ sticks) chilled unsalted butter, in ½-inch slices
1	egg, lightly beaten
2	teaspoons fresh lemon juice
4 to 5	tablespoons ice water

Stir the flour and salt together. Cut the butter into the flour until the mixture resembles coarse crumbs.

With a fork, stir the egg, lemon juice, and 2 tablespoons of the ice water together. Sprinkle the liquid over the flour mixture and mix just until the pastry holds together, adding more water if needed. Knead the dough in the bowl for 2 or 3 strokes—just until the dough makes a smooth ball. Cover and chill for 30 minutes or until firm, and use as directed in recipes.

FLAKY COTTAGE CHEESE PASTRY

Makes enough dough for 1 double-crust pie

This is a simple and delicious butter pastry that is so flaky that it resembles puff pastry in texture.

- **2   cups all-purpose flour**
- **1   cup (2 sticks) chilled butter, in ½-inch slices**
- **1   cup cream-style cottage cheese**

Measure the flour into a bowl. Cut in the butter until it resembles very coarse crumbs. Stir in the cottage cheese and blend with a fork until a dough forms. Knead just until the dough is blended, 5 to 10 strokes. Cover and chill for 30 minutes or until ready to use.

SOUR CREAM PASTRY

Makes enough dough for 1 double-crust pie

This pastry is reminiscent of a baking powder biscuit dough, even though it is rolled thin. It goes well with the flavors of vegetable fillings.

- 1½   **cups all-purpose flour**
- ½   **teaspoon salt**
- 2   **teaspoons baking powder**
- ½   **cup (1 stick) chilled unsalted butter, in ½-inch slices**
- 1   **cup sour cream**

In a large bowl mix the flour, salt, and baking powder. Cut in the butter until it resembles very coarse crumbs. Stir in the sour cream to make a stiff pastry. Wrap and chill the dough about 30 minutes.

CORN BREAD CRUST

Makes enough for 1 pie topping

This is a quick, stir-together crust that makes a soft, corn bread–like topping. It's great for an old-fashioned pot pie, chili, or chicken or turkey casserole.

1   cup all-purpose flour
1   cup stone-ground white or yellow cornmeal
2   tablespoons sugar
1   tablespoon baking powder
1   teaspoon salt
1   egg, lightly beaten
1   cup milk
3   tablespoons vegetable oil

Measure the flour, cornmeal, sugar, baking powder, and salt into a mixing bowl; blend well.

Stir together the egg, milk, and oil and mix into the dry ingredients just until combined. Cover and chill.

CORNMEAL PASTRY

Makes enough pastry for 1 double-crust pie

There's a tiny bit of crunch to this pastry. It works with almost any pie, but is especially good with Chicken and Spinach Pie (page 42) and as an alternative crust for any meat pie.

1⅔	cups all-purpose flour
¼	cup stone-ground yellow or white cornmeal
1	teaspoon salt
¾	cup (1½ sticks) chilled unsalted butter, in ½-inch slices
1	egg, lightly beaten
2	teaspoons white vinegar
2 to 3	tablespoons ice water

Stir together the flour, cornmeal, and salt. Cut in the butter until the mixture resembles coarse crumbs. With a fork, stir the egg, vinegar, and 1 tablespoon of the ice water together. Add the liquid to the flour mixture, stirring with a fork just until the pastry is moist enough to hold together. Add more ice water, if necessary, a tablespoon at a time. Knead in the bowl for 2 or 3 strokes, just until the dough makes a smooth ball. Wrap the pastry and chill for 30 minutes or until ready to use.

QUICK-RISING
PIZZA DOUGH

Makes enough dough for one 12-inch pizza

If you have only regular active-dry yeast on hand and wish a speedier rising, just double the yeast in this recipe.

1	**package (2½ tablespoons) quick-rise active dry yeast**
½	**tablespoon sugar**
¾	**cup warm water (105°–115°F)**
½	**teaspoon salt**
1½ to 2	**cups all-purpose flour**
1	**tablespoon olive oil**

In a large mixing bowl, dissolve the yeast and the sugar in the warm water. Let it stand for 5 minutes, or until the mixture foams. Stir in the salt, 1½ cups of the flour, and the olive oil, mixing until smooth. Turn the dough out onto a work surface and knead, adding more flour as necessary, until the dough is smooth and satiny. The kneading may also be done in a food processor using the dough hook. Let the dough rise until puffy, about 30 minutes.

ACKNOWLEDGMENTS

If a tree falls in the forest and there is nobody there to hear it, does it make a sound?

This classic question, applied to the life of anyone who loves to create great food away from the mainstream, has a definite answer. No. It is only when a food writer has a receiving ear that books such as this can be produced. That important ear for me is a person who has become a good friend in the past few years, my encouraging agent Elise Goodman. This book is one result, and I am grateful.

Special thanks to Katie Workman, my enthusiastic and patient editor at Clarkson Potter. Thanks to Pam Krauss, too, for her support.

I would also like to thank a group of my friends who helped with the initial testing of these recipes: Marcia, Marj, Mary, Peggy, Kay, Lois, Ruth, Doris, Avis, Brenda, Annette, Ann, Beth, Jean, Gudrun, Helen, Erna, Norma Jean, Nancy, and Cecile. The result of the testing was a great party, but alas, I regret that we didn't get to include the Lutefisk Pie in this book.

INDEX